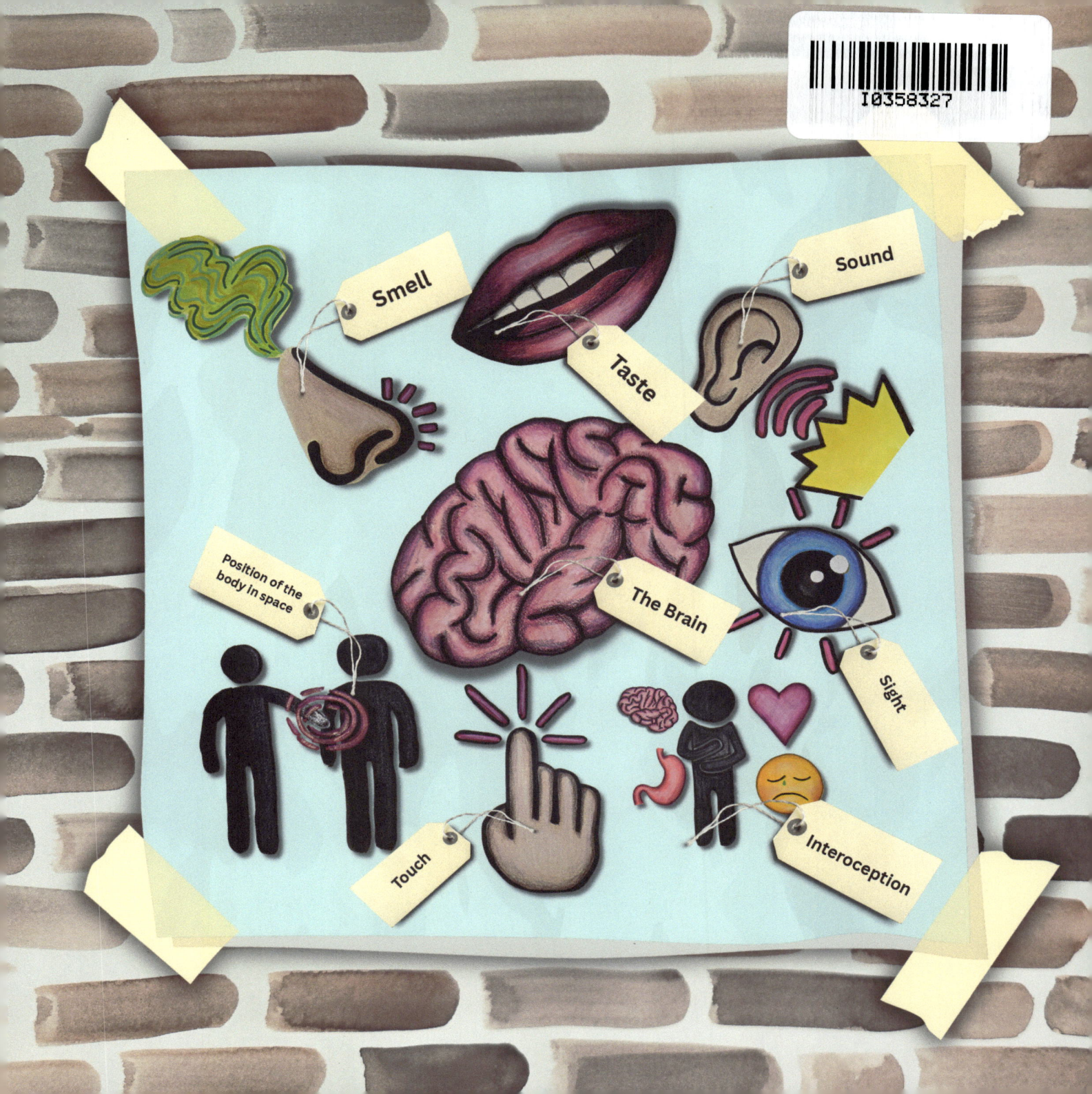

Busy Brains for Boys:
Supporting Executive Functioning and Neurodiversity in the Classroom

Written and Illustrated by Tenille Dowe

Copyright © 2025 Tenille Dowe

All rights reserved. No part of this book may be reproduced in any manner whatsoever without prior written permission of the publisher.

First Printing, 2025

Published by Creative Heart Connection
www.creativeheartconnection.com

ISBN 978-1-7641624-0-1

Busy Brains

Supporting Executive Functioning and Neurodiversity in the Classroom

For Boys

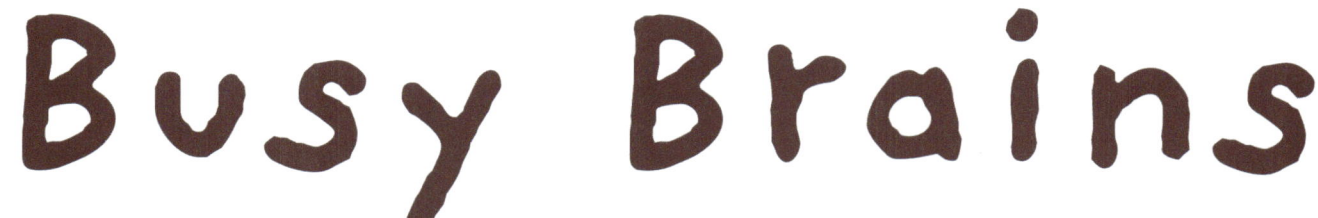

Written and Illustrated by Tenille Dowe

His bedroom is a sanctuary
where he can explore.
Free from the chaos of school,
it's a place to restore.

His special interests bloom without any rush.
In a world where his family
knows what he likes so much.

With love and comfort,
anxiety and overwhelm is chased away.
A predictable haven where he feels okay.

In a bustling corridor where he roams,
feeling anxious because he's not at home.

The noise and crowd are quite a fright,
turning his world into a dizzying and
overwhelming plight.

With compassion, support and a few things
done differently,
things will feel better and right.

In a busy classroom it's often too loud,
noise-cancelling headphones feel like a cloud.

Sensory overload can be tough,
where every sound seems to be just too much.

Headphones can help in creating calm,
a quiet space, allowing him to focus on his own.

It's not just about silence, it's about finding peace,
helping him manage when
sensory challenges increase.

So, when the world feels too noisy and bright,
these headphones can make things feel just right.

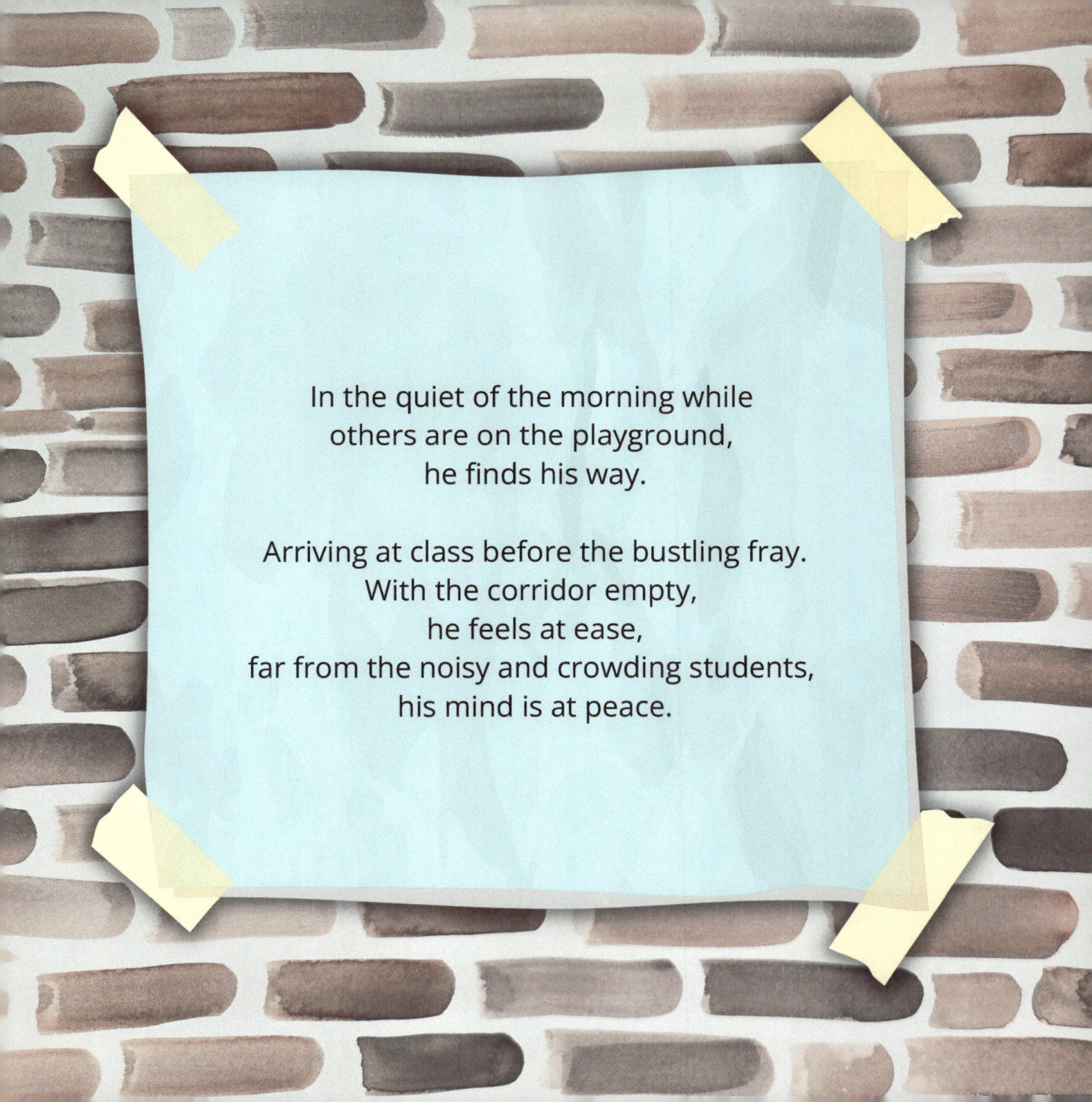

In the quiet of the morning while
others are on the playground,
he finds his way.

Arriving at class before the bustling fray.
With the corridor empty,
he feels at ease,
far from the noisy and crowding students,
his mind is at peace.

When he enters the classroom, his bag spills wide,
amidst the chaos and increasing anxiety.
He doesn't know where to start inside.

Though papers and books may scatter and stray,
he needs a schedule to find his way.

His world appears unorganised and cluttered.

Order brings peace,
and with a clear plan,
his worries release.

In the classroom, success began
when the rules and routine were clear.

For him, organisation brought
a lightness and cheer.

With a tidy desk, focus would flow,
and learning became easier,
allowing him to grow.

In this structured space,
he found his stride.
Thriving with confidence, side by side.

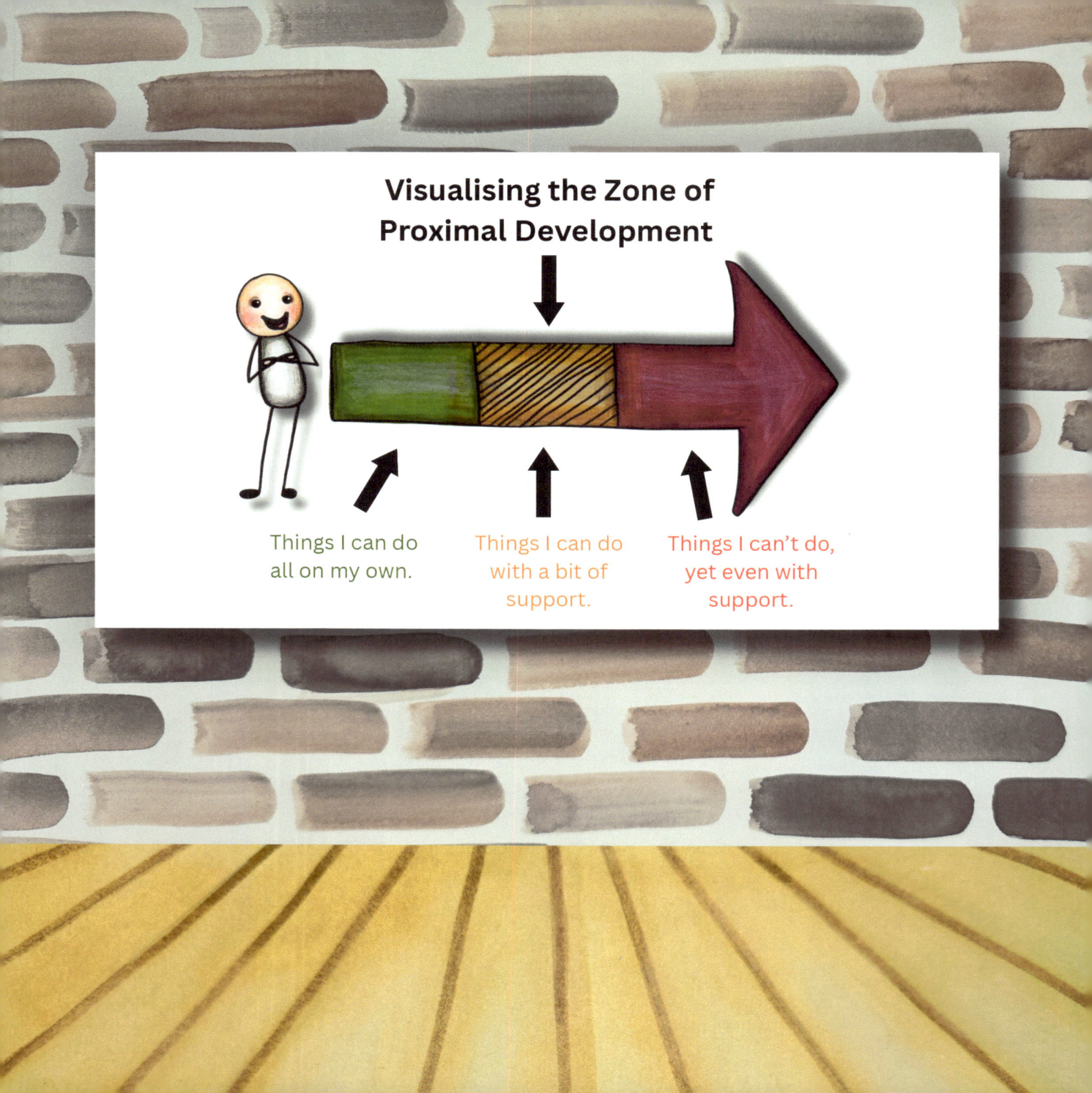

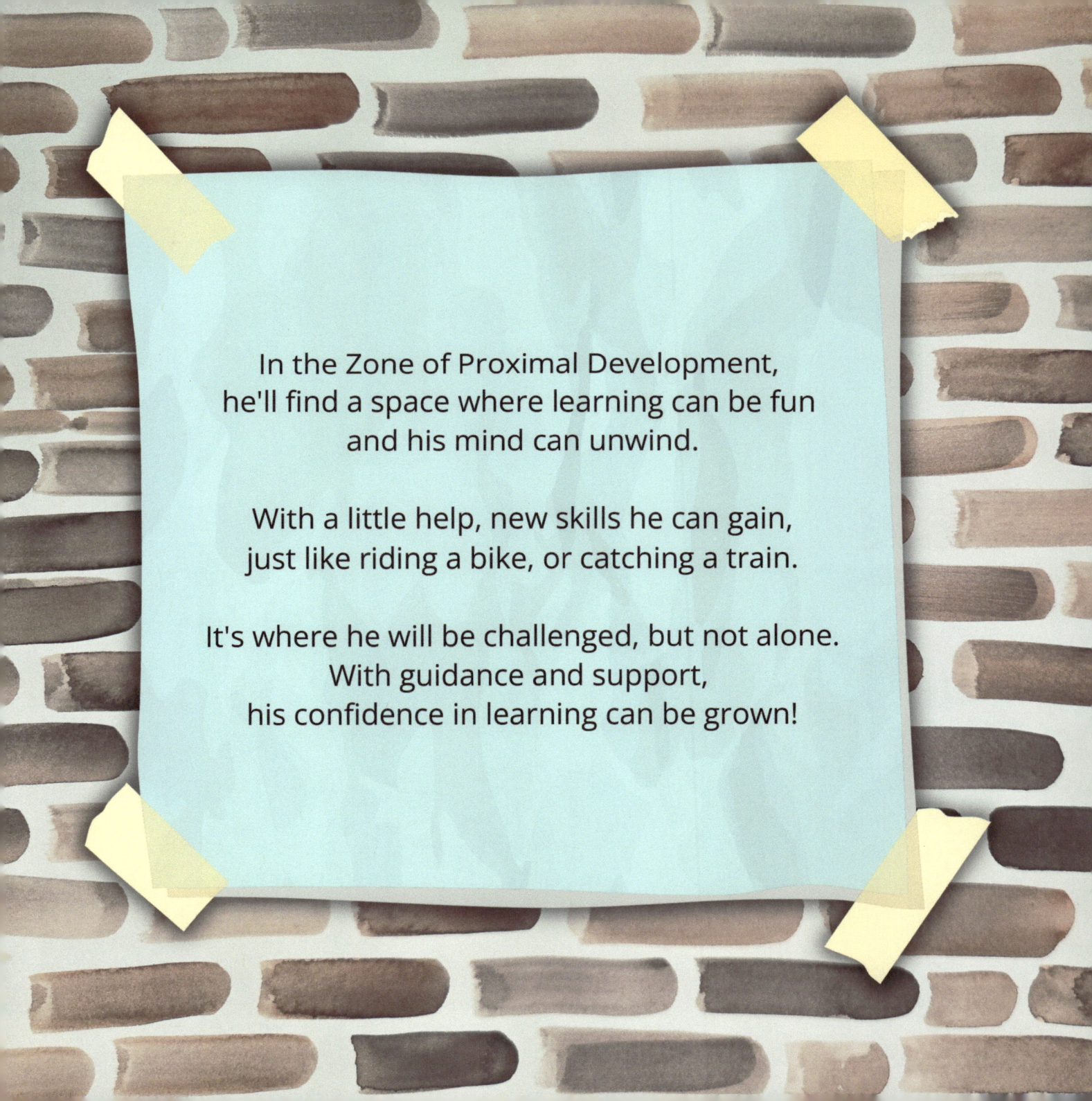

In the Zone of Proximal Development,
he'll find a space where learning can be fun
and his mind can unwind.

With a little help, new skills he can gain,
just like riding a bike, or catching a train.

It's where he will be challenged, but not alone.
With guidance and support,
his confidence in learning can be grown!

In his class, a traffic light system is the key.
Where students use colours to set their learning free.

Red means you're stuck,
even with help you can't proceed.

Yellow is just right,
where a little support is all you'll need.

Green shines bright for tasks you can do
without help and at great speed.

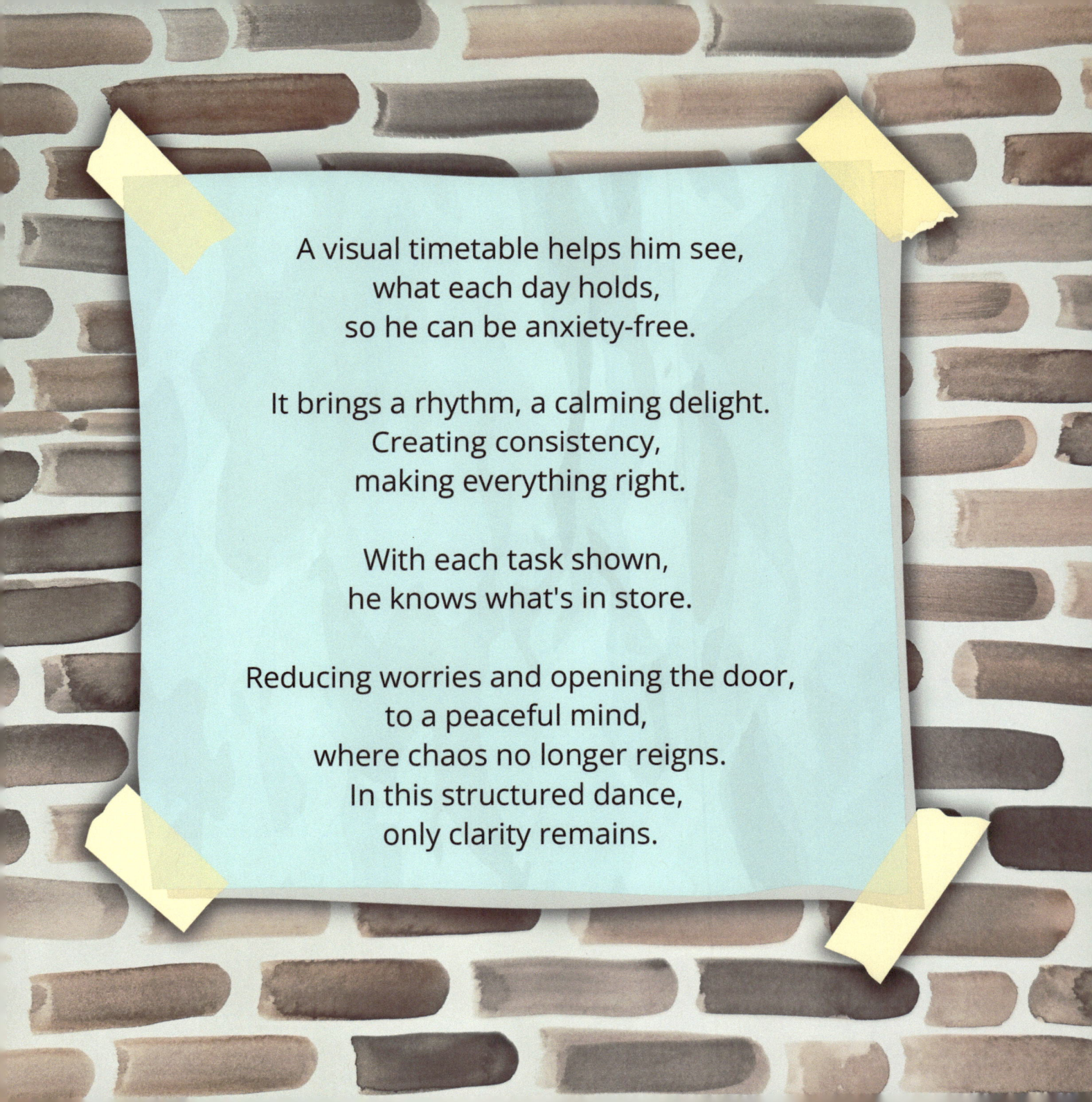

A visual timetable helps him see,
what each day holds,
so he can be anxiety-free.

It brings a rhythm, a calming delight.
Creating consistency,
making everything right.

With each task shown,
he knows what's in store.

Reducing worries and opening the door,
to a peaceful mind,
where chaos no longer reigns.
In this structured dance,
only clarity remains.

Interoception is the sense that lets you see,
when you're hungry,
thirsty, or need to pee!

It helps you know when you need a break,
like when your tummy rumbles,
or your brain feels like it might ache.

At school, it guides you,
keeping your needs in sight.

Showing when to pause
and make things right!

In the classroom's bustling pace,
he sometimes feels out of place.

Interoception shouts,
his heart is beating so fast,
as if it was in a frantic race.

Struggling with the task at hand,
frustration starts to show.

Overwhelmed by the feeling of failure,
his patience runs low.

In his mind, he searches for calm,
hoping the chaos will go.

In the classroom, when he can't start a task,
he feels stuck and trapped.
His head lowers on his desk,
all his options seem sapped.

Eyes closed, tuning into his inner state,
sensing and feeling his own heartbeat
as his thoughts circulate.

During the hardest lesson,
he wishes for a way to feel less
confused and dazed.

In the classroom, when things start to feel tight,
he remembers the system:
Green, yellow and red light.

Yellow means he needs help,
so in future he will raise his hand high.

He still needs reminders from the teacher,
no need to be shy.

With the traffic light system in mind,
he can start to feel safe.
He can ask for help,
his learning can take flight.

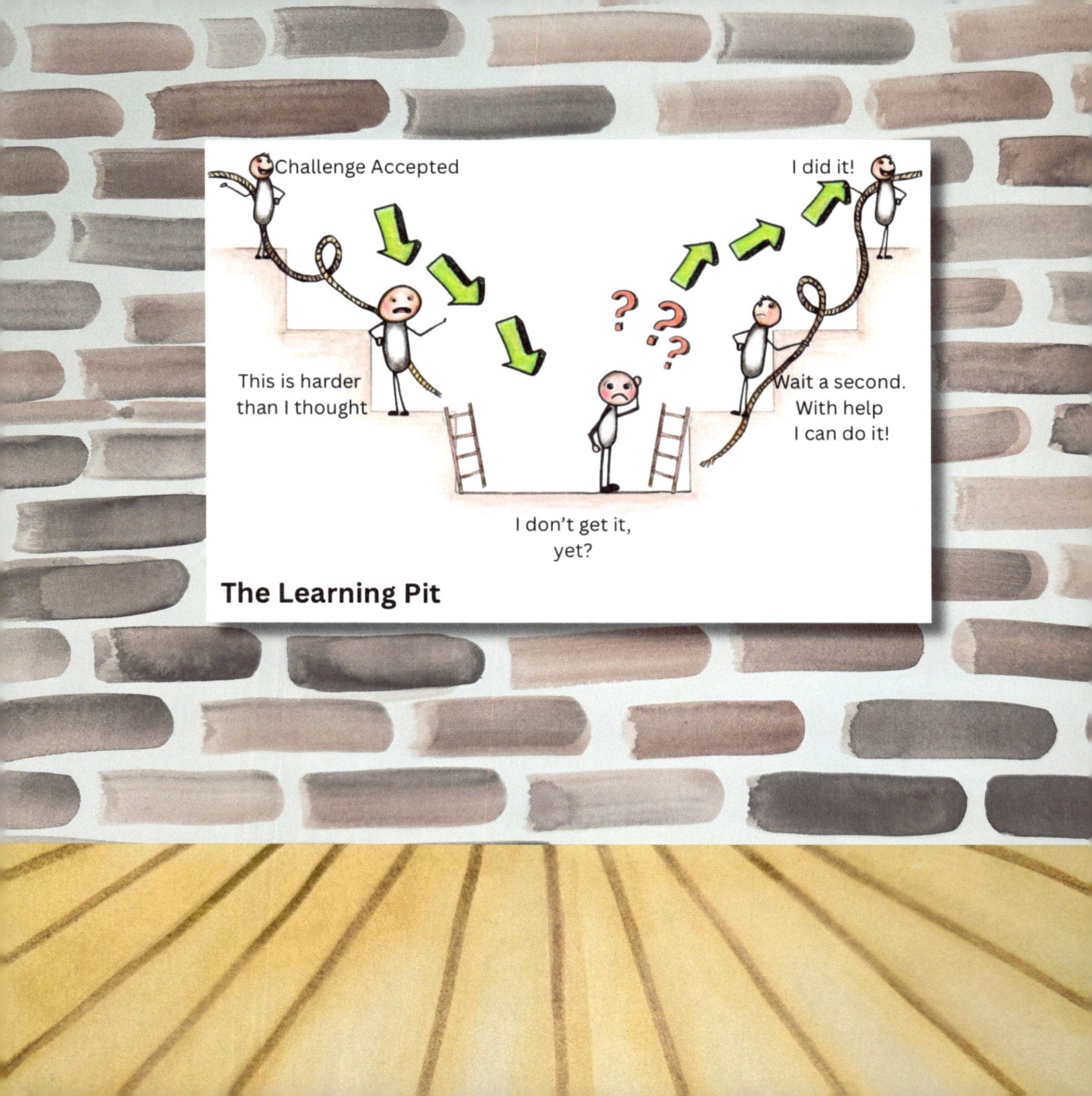

His teacher calmly told him a story.....

"Imagine you're on an adventure,
deep in the Learning Pit.
Where challenges are hard, but you don't quit.
You take a leap, though the climb seemed steep,
and found it tougher than you did at first peep.

With your teacher's help, you made a start,
using a checklist, you play your part.

Step by step, you work with zest,
and now you're moving towards doing your best.
Keep going, you're on the right track,
with effort and grit, there's no turning back".

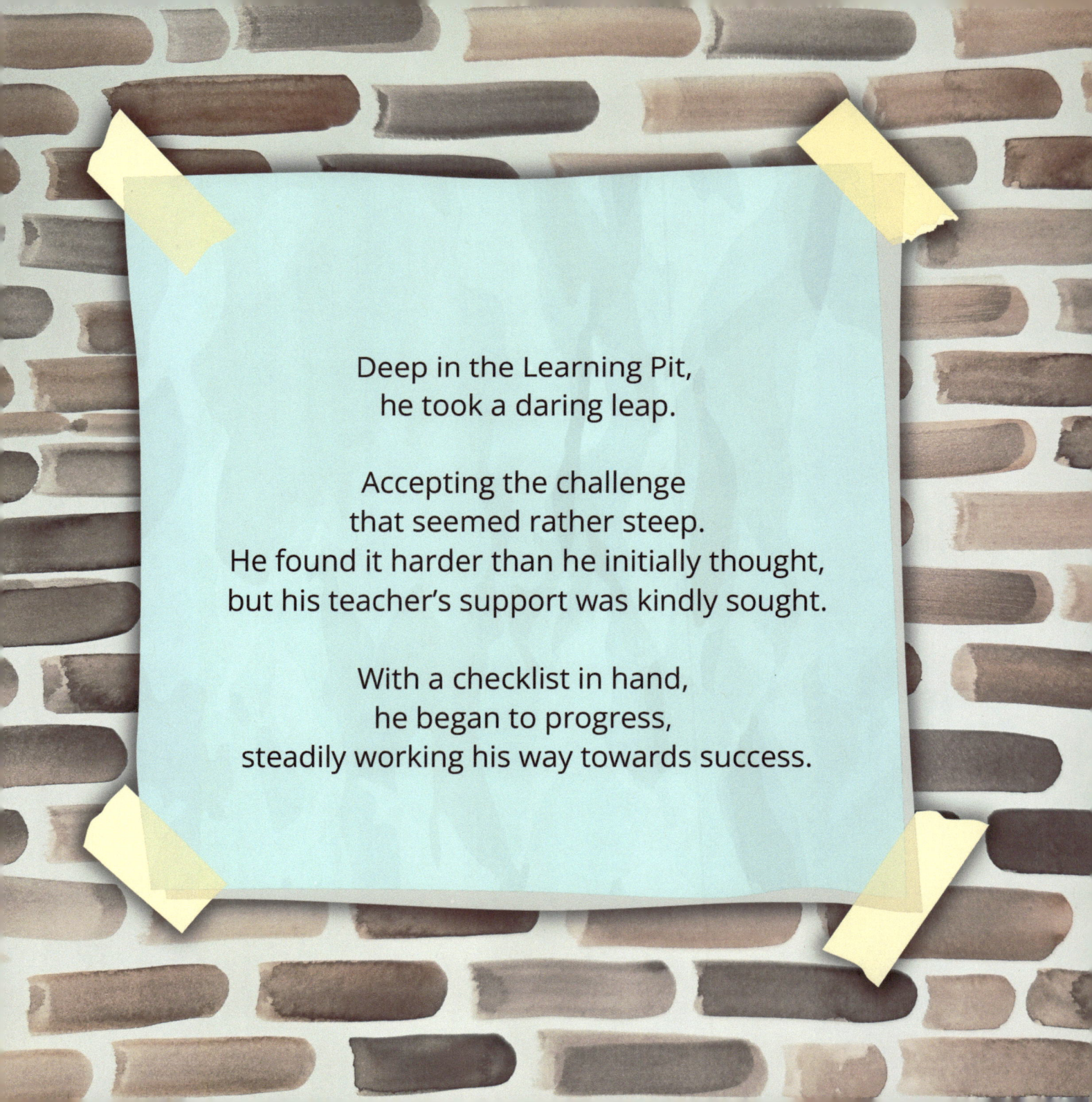

Deep in the Learning Pit,
he took a daring leap.

Accepting the challenge
that seemed rather steep.
He found it harder than he initially thought,
but his teacher's support was kindly sought.

With a checklist in hand,
he began to progress,
steadily working his way towards success.

You took a daring leap into the Learning Pit,
facing challenges that seemed quite steep.

With your teacher's support,
a checklist in hand,
you found your way.

Growing stronger with each passing day.
You conquered the pit
with a triumphant cheer.

Your success is well-earned,
that's perfectly clear!

At school and in the classroom,
he finds his stride with supports
that are just right.

Adjusting to challenges,
he's ready to take flight.

A calming corner awaits
when he needs to refocus his mind.
Helping him regroup, leaving worries behind.

With these adjustments in place,
his potential's truly unconfined.

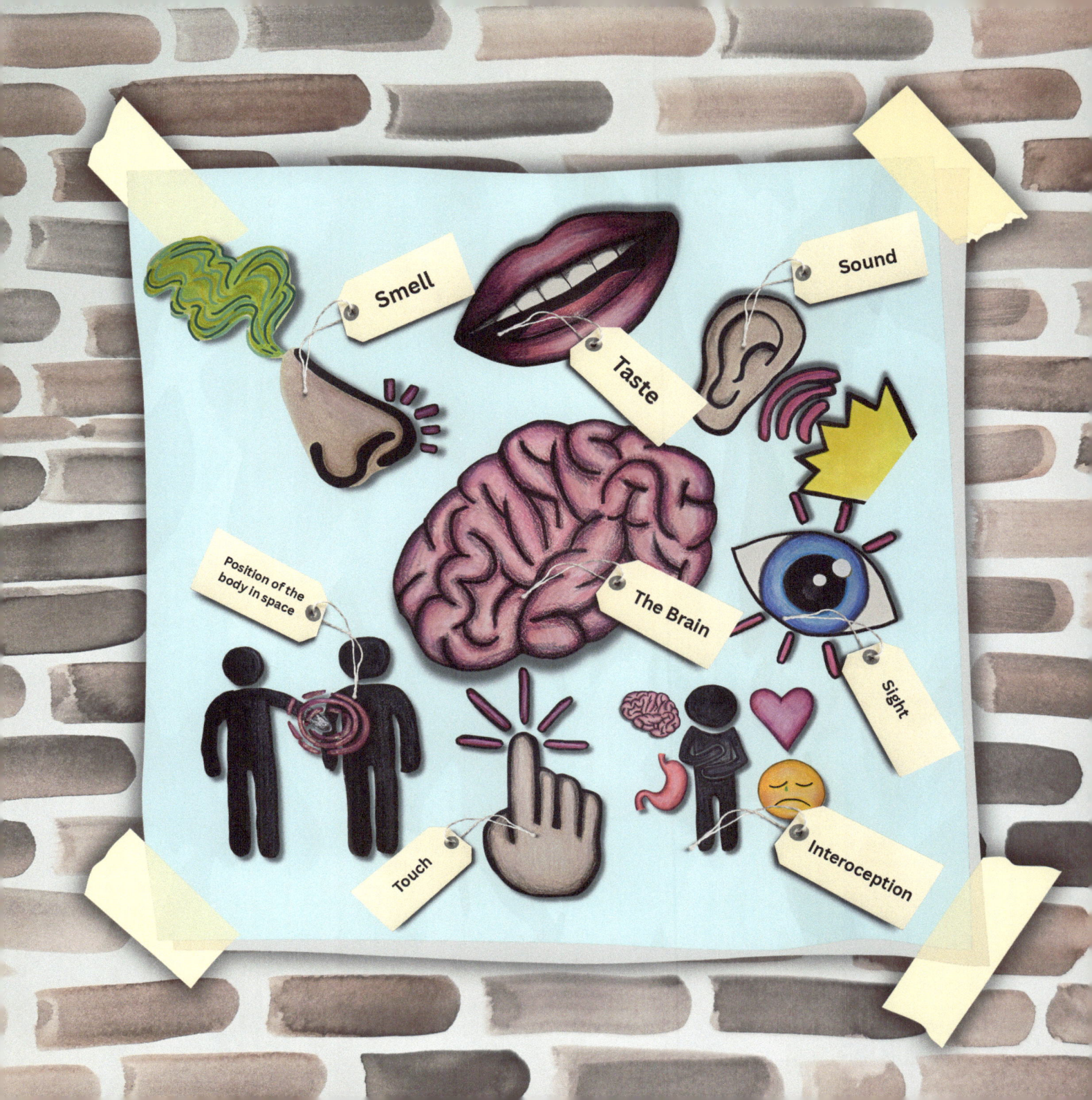

www.ingramcontent.com/pod-product-compliance
Lightning Source LLC
Chambersburg PA
CBHW041110070526
44583CB00003B/127